Worship BAND PLAY-ALONG

KEYBOARD EDITION Volume 2

Here I Am to Worship

Recorded and produced by Jim Reith at BeatHouse Music, Milwaukee, WI

Lead Vocals by Tonia Emrich and Jim Reith
Background Vocals by Jim Reith, Janna Wolf and Joy Palisoc Bach
Guitars by Mike DeRose and Joe Gorman
Bass by Chris Kringel
Keyboard by Kurt Cowling
Drums by Del Bennett

ISBN 978-1-4234-1717-0

HAL•LEONARD® CORPORATION

7777 W. BLUEMOUND RD. P.O. BOX 13819 MILWAUKEE, WI 53213

Visit Hal Leonard Online at
www.halleonard.com

Come, Now Is the Time to Worship

Words and Music by Brian Doerksen

just as you are, _____ to wor - ship.

Come, just as you are, _____ be - fore _____ your _____ God. Come.

B Chorus

One day ev -'ry tongue will con - fess _____ You are God. _ One day ev -'ry knee _ will bow. _

Still, the great-est treas-ure re-mains _ for those _ who glad-ly choose _ You now. _____ Come, now is the time _ to wor — ship. Come, _____ now is the time _ to give _____ your _____

heart. Come, just as you are, _____ to wor-

-ship. Come,

just as you are, _____ be - fore _____ your _____ God.

D Chorus

Come. One day ev - 'ry tongue will con - fess _

You are God. One day ev-'ry knee will bow.

Still, the great-est treas-ure re-mains for those who glad-ly choose You now.

E Chorus

And one day ev-'ry tongue will con-fess You are God.

One day ev-'ry knee will bow. Still, the great-est treas-ure re-mains for those _ who glad \- ly choose _ You now. _

_ Come, now is the time _ to wor -

\- ship. Come,

now is the time _ to give _ your _ heart.

Come,   just as you are, _____ to wor -

ship.   Come,   just as you are, _____ be - fore _

Outro

_ your _____ God.   Come.

Come.   Come.

Give Us Clean Hands

Words and Music by Charlie Hall

give us pure hearts. Let us not lift our souls to an-oth-

-er. Give us clean hands, give us pure hearts. Let us not

lift our souls to an-oth - er. And God, let us be

a gen-er-a-tion that seeks, that seeks Your face, O God of Ja-

-cob. And God, let us be _____ a gen-er-a-tion that seeks, ____ that seeks Your face, ____

____ O ____ God ____ of Ja - cob. _____

C **Verse**

We bow our hearts, we bend our knees. O Spir-it, come make us hum-

ble. We turn our eyes from e - vil things.

O Lord, we cast down our i - dols. Give us clean hands, give us pure hearts.

Let us not lift our souls to an - oth - er. Give us clean hands,

give us pure hearts. Let us not lift our souls to an - oth -

- er. And God, let us be a gen - er - a - tion that seeks, that seeks Your face,

O — God — of Ja - cob. And God, let us be —

— a gen - er - a - tion that seeks, — that seeks Your face, — O — God — of Ja -

E Tag

- cob. — We bow our hearts,

we bend our knees. O Spir - it, come make us hum - ble.

Hear Our Praises

Words and Music by Reuben Morgan

May in-jus - tice bow ____ to Je - sus ____

as the peo - ple turn ____ to pray. __

B Chorus

____ From the moun - tain ____

____ to the val - ley, ____ hear our

May our light ___ shine in ___ the dark-

-ness ___ as we walk ___

___ be - fore ___ the cross. ___

May Your glo - ry fill _____ the whole _____ earth _____

as the wa - ter o'er _____ the seas. _

D Chorus

From the moun - tain _____

to the val - ley, _____ hear our

Am   Em7   F

prais - es _____ rise to You. _____

Gsus   C   G/B

___ From the heav - ens _____ to the

F/A   Am   Em7

na - tions, _____ hear the sing - ing _____ fill the

F   Gsus   C

air. _____ Hal - le -

Chorus

moun - tain _____ to the val - ley, _____

_____ hear our prais - es _____ rise to

You. _____ From the heav - ens _____

_____ to the na - tions, _____ hear the

Am   Em7   F   Gsus

sing - ing _____ fill the air. _____ From the

G **Chorus**

C   G/B   F/A

moun - tain _____ to the val - ley, _____

Am   Em7

_____ hear our prais - es _____ rise to

F   Gsus   C

You. _____ From the heav - ens _____

to the na - tions, _____ hear the

sing - ing _____ fill the air. _____

Outro

rit.

Here I Am to Worship

Words and Music by Tim Hughes

You're al-to-geth-er love-ly, al-to-geth-er

wor-thy, al-to-geth-er won-der-ful to me.___

Light of the world, You stepped down in-to dark-ness,

o-pened my eyes, let me___ see.

I Give You My Heart

Words and Music by Reuben Morgan

I wor-ship You.

All I have with-in me, I give You praise.

All that I a-dore is in You.

B Chorus

Lord, I give You my heart,

I give You my __ soul. __ I live for You a-lone. __

__ Ev-'ry breath that I __ take, __ ev-'ry mo-ment I'm __ a-wake, __ Lord,

have Your way in me. __

C Verse

This is my __ de - si - re, to hon - or

Ev-'ry breath that I ___ take, ___ ev'ry mo-ment I'm ___ a - wake, ___ Lord,

F Outro

have Your way in me. ___

Have Your way in me. ___

rit.

Let Everything That Has Breath

Words and Music by Matt Redman

ev -'ry - thing _ that, ev -'ry - thing _ that has breath praise the Lord. _

_ Let ev -'ry - thing _ that, ev -'ry - thing _ that, ev -'ry - thing _ that

has breath praise the Lord. ____

B Verse 1

Praise _ You in the morn - ing, _ praise _ You in the eve - ning, _

praise __ You when I'm young and when I'm old.

Praise __ You when I'm laugh - ing, __ praise __ You when I'm griev - ing, __

praise __ You ev -'ry sea - son of the soul. _____ If

C Pre-Chorus 1

we could see how much You're worth, Your pow'r, Your might, Your

has breath praise the Lord. _____

E **Verse 2**

Praise _ You in the heav - ens, _ join - ing with the an - gels, _

prais - ing You for - ev - er and a day.

Praise _ You on the earth now, _ join - ing with cre - a - tion, _

call - ing all the na - tions to Your praise. If

F Pre-Chorus 2

they could see how much You're worth, Your pow'r, Your might, Your

end - less love, then sure - ly they would nev - er cease to

G Chorus

praise. _____ Let ev - 'ry - thing _ that,

You're Worthy of My Praise

Words and Music by David Ruis

You a-lone __ I long __ to __ wor - ship, You a-lone __ are

wor - thy of __ my __ praise. __

C **Verse 2**

I will bow down

(I will bow down) and hail You __ as __ King (and hail You __ as __ King).

You a-lone _ I long _ to _ wor-ship, You a-lone _ are

wor-thy of _ my _ praise. _____

F **Tag**

You're wor-thy of _ my _ praise. _____

You're wor-thy of _ my _ praise.

You Alone

Words and Music by Jack Parker and David Crowder

With a lilt (♩. = ca. 50)

Intro

You are the only one I need, I bow all of me at Your feet, I worship You a-lone.

You _____ a - lone __ are __ Sav - ior and You _____ a - lone __

__ are _____ God. _____

C **Verse**

You _____ are _____ the

on - ly one I _____ need, _____ I bow all of me at Your __

D **Chorus**

You _____ a - lone __ are __ Fa - ther and You _____ a - lone _

__ are __ good. You _____ a - lone __ are __ Sav - ior and You _

_____ a - lone __ are __ God. I'm a - live, _ I'm a - live, _

E **Bridge**

__ I'm a - live, _ I'm a - live. I'm a - live, _ I'm a - live, __ I'm a - live, _ I'm a - live.

I'm a-live,__ I'm a-live,__ I'm a-live,__ I'm a-live. I'm a-live,__ I'm a-live.__

F Chorus

You _____ a-lone __ are __ Fa - ther and You__

a - lone __ are __ good. You _____ a - lone __

____ are __ Sav - ior and You _____ a - lone __ are _____ God.

You _____ a - lone __ are __ Fa - ther and You _____ a - lone _

__ are __ good. You _____ a - lone __ are __ Sav - ior and You _

a - lone __ are _____ God. _____

Outro

slight rit.

COME, NOW IS THE TIME TO WORSHIP

BRIAN DOERKSEN

Key of **D Major**, 4/4

INTRO:

D   G/D D   G/D

VERSE:

D   G/D   D
Come, now is the time to wor -   ship

A   Em7   D/F♯   G
Come, now is the time to give   your   heart

D   G/D   D
Come, just as you are, to wor -   ship

A   Em7 D/F♯   G
Come, just as you are, before   your   God

D
Come

CHORUS:

G   D
One day ev'ry tongue will confess You are God

G   D
One day ev'ry knee will bow

G   Bm
Still, the greatest treasure remains for those

      Em7   Asus   A
Who gladly choose You now

(REPEAT VERSE)

(REPEAT CHORUS 2X)

(REPEAT VERSE)

OUTRO:

   D   G/D D   G/D D (hold)
(Come)   Come   Come

GIVE US CLEAN HANDS

CHARLIE HALL

Key of **G Major**, 4/4

INTRO:

G   D   G/B C   G

VERSE:

G   D   G/B
   We bow our hearts, we bend our knees
C   G
   O Spirit, come make us humble
G   D   G/B
   We turn our eyes from evil things
C
   O Lord, we cast down our idols

CHORUS:

C/D   G   D
Give us clean hands, give us pure hearts
       Em   D   G
Let us not lift our souls to another
              G   D
Give us clean hands, give us pure hearts
       Em   D   G
Let us not lift our souls to another
              G   D
And God, let us be a generation that seeks
         Em   D   G
That seeks Your face, O God of Jacob
              G   D
And God, let us be a generation that seeks
         Em   D   Csus2 (2 bars)
That seeks Your face, O God of Jacob

(REPEAT VERSE & CHORUS)

TAG:

G   D   G/B
   We bow our hearts, we bend our knees
C   G (hold)
   O Spirit, come make us humble

HEAR OUR PRAISES

REUBEN MORGAN

Key of **C Major, 4/4**

INTRO:

C   Csus   C   Csus

VERSE 1:

C   Csus   C   G/B
   May our homes be filled with dancing

Am   F   Gsus   G
   May our streets be filled with joy

C   Csus   C   G/B
   May injustice bow to Jesus

Am   F   Gsus   G
   As the people turn to pray

CHORUS:

       C   G/B   F/A
From the mountain   to the valley

      Am   Em7   F   Gsus
Hear our praises   rise to You

       C   G/B   F/A
From the heavens   to the nations

      Am   Em7   F   Gsus
Hear the singing   fill the air

(REPEAT INTRO)

VERSE 2:

C   Csus   C   G/B
   May our light shine in the darkness

Am   F   Gsus   G
   As we walk before the cross

C   Csus   C   G/B
   May Your glory fill the whole earth

Am   F   Gsus   G
   As the water o'er the seas

(REPEAT CHORUS)

TRANSITION TO BRIDGE:

C (2 bars)

BRIDGE (2X):

   F   Dm7   Am   Em7
Hallelujah,   hallelujah

   F   Dm7   Gsus   G
Hallelujah,   hallelujah

(REPEAT CHORUS 2X)

OUTRO:

C   Csus   C   Csus   C (hold)

HERE I AM TO WORSHIP

TIM HUGHES

Key of **D Major**, 4/4

INTRO:

D A Em7 D A G

VERSE 1:

D   A   Em7
Light of the world, You stepped down into darkness

D   A   G
Opened my eyes, let me see

D   A   Em7
Beauty that made this heart adore You

D   A   G (2 bars)
Hope of a life spent with You

CHORUS:

                D   A
Here I am to worship, here I am to bow down

              D/F♯   G
Here I am to say that You're my God

                 D   A
You're altogether lovely, altogether worthy

              D/F♯   G
Altogether wonderful to me

VERSE 2:

D   A   Em7
King of all days, oh, so highly exalted

D   A   G
Glorious in heaven above

D   A   Em7
Humbly You came to the earth You created

D   A   G (1 bar)
All for love's sake became poor

(REPEAT CHORUS)

BRIDGE (2X):

          A/C♯   D/F♯   G
And I'll never know   how much it cost

     A/C♯   D/F♯ G
To see my sin   upon that cross

(REPEAT CHORUS 2X)

TAG:

D   A   Em7
Light of the world, You stepped down into darkness

D   A   G (hold)
Opened my eyes, let me see

I GIVE YOU MY HEART

REUBEN MORGAN

Key of **D Major, 4/4**

INTRO:

Gmaj7   A/G   F♯m7   Bm7
Gmaj7   A/G   F♯m7   G/A

VERSE:

D   A/C♯ Bm7
This is my de - sire

    G   D   A
To hon - or You

Bm7   A/C♯   D
Lord, with all   my   heart

        Cmaj7   G   A
I worship You

D   A/C♯ Bm7
All I have with - in me

  G   D   A
I give You praise

Bm7   A/C♯   D
All that I a - dore

    Cmaj7   G   A
Is in You

CHORUS:

D   A
Lord, I give You my heart

         Em7
I give You my soul

 G/A
I live for You alone

D   A/C♯
Ev'ry breath that I take

        Em7
Ev'ry moment I'm awake

   G/A   (**Gmaj7   A/G   G/A**)
Lord, have Your way in me

(REPEAT VERSE)

(REPEAT CHORUS 2X)

OUTRO:

Gmaj7   A/G   F♯m7   Bm7
Gmaj7   A/G   F♯m7   G/A   D (hold)

LET EVERYTHING THAT HAS BREATH

MATT REDMAN

Key of **E Major, 4/4**

INTRO:

E5   E5/D♯   C♯m7   Asus2 A/B

E5   E5/D♯   C♯m7   Asus2 A/B   F♯m7 (2 bars)

CHORUS:

E5   E5/D♯
Let everything that, everything that

C♯m7   Asus2   A/B
Everything that has breath praise the Lord

E5   E5/D♯
Let everything that, everything that

C♯m7   Asus2   A/B   F♯m7 (2 bars)
Everything that has breath praise the Lord

VERSE 1:

E5
Praise You in the morning

E5/D♯
Praise You in the evening

C♯m7   Asus2
Praise You when I'm young and when I'm old

E5
Praise You when I'm laughing

E5/D♯
Praise You when I'm grieving

C♯m7   Asus2
Praise You ev'ry season of the soul

PRE-CHORUS 1:

 F♯m7   E/G♯
If we could see how much You're worth

    F♯m7   E/G♯
Your pow'r, Your might, Your endless love

     F♯m7   E/G♯   A A/B
Then surely we would never cease to praise

(REPEAT CHORUS)

VERSE 2:

E5
Praise You in the heavens

E5/D♯
Joining with the angels

C♯m7   Asus2
Praising You forever and a day

E5
Praise You on the earth now

E5/D♯
Joining with creation

C♯m7   Asus2
Calling all the nations to Your praise

PRE-CHORUS 2:

 F♯m7   E/G♯
If they could see how much You're worth

    F♯m7   E/G♯
Your pow'r, Your might, Your endless love

     F♯m7   E/G♯   A A/B
Then surely they would never cease to praise

(REPEAT CHORUS 3X)

END ON E

YOU ALONE

JACK PARKER and DAVID CROWDER

Key of **E Major, 6/8**

INTRO:

E   E/G♯   Asus2

E   E/G♯   Asus2

VERSE:

E   E/G♯   Asus2
You   are   the only one I

E   E/G♯   Asus2
Need,   I   bow all of me at Your

E   E/G♯   Asus2   E E/G♯ Asus2
Feet,   I   worship You alone

E   E/G♯   Asus2
You   have   given me more than

E E/G♯   Asus2
I   could   ever have wanted, and

E E/G♯   Asus2   E E/G♯ Asus2
I   want   to give You my heart and my soul

CHORUS:

E   E/G♯   Asus2
You   alone are Father

        E   E/G♯   Asus2   B
And You   alone are good

E   E/G♯   Asus2
You   alone are Savior

        E   E/G♯ Asus2   (B)
And You   alone are God

INTERLUDE:

E   E/G♯   Asus2

E   E/G♯   Asus2

(REPEAT VERSE & CHORUS)

BRIDGE:

E   E/G♯   Asus2
I'm alive, I'm alive, I'm alive, I'm alive

E   E/G♯   Asus2
I'm alive, I'm alive, I'm alive, I'm alive

E   E/G♯   Asus2
I'm alive, I'm alive, I'm alive, I'm alive

E   E/G♯   Asus2   B
I'm alive, I'm alive

(REPEAT CHORUS 2X)

OUTRO:

E   E/G♯   Asus2

E   E/G♯   Asus2   E (hold)

YOU'RE WORTHY OF MY PRAISE

DAVID RUIS

Key of **E Major**, 4/4

INTRO:

E   D/E

VERSE 1:

E   *Echo:*
I will worship (*I will worship*)

     D/E
With all of my heart (*with all of my heart*)

A
I will praise You (*I will praise You*)

       E   F#m7   Bsus B
With all of my strength (*all my strength*)

E
I will seek You (*I will seek You*)

D/E
All of my days (*all of my days*)

A
I will follow (*I will follow*)

E   F#m7   Bsus B
All of Your ways (*all Your ways*)

CHORUS:

E   B
I will give You all my worship

F#m7   A   Bsus B
I will give You all my praise

E   B
You alone I long to worship

F#m7   A Bsus B   E   D/E
You alone are worthy of   my praise

VERSE 2:

E
I will bow down (*I will bow down*)

     D/E
And hail You as King (*and hail You as King*)

A
I will serve You (*I will serve You*)

           E   F#m7   Bsus B
Give You ev'rything (*give You ev'rything*)

E
I will lift up (*I will lift up*)

     D/E
My eyes to Your throne (*my eyes to Your throne*)

A
I will trust You (*I will trust You*)

E   F#m7   Bsus B
Trust You alone (*trust in You alone*)

(REPEAT CHORUS 2X)

TAG:

        A Bsus B   E   D/E
You're worthy of   my praise

        A Bsus B   E (hold)
You're worthy of   my praise